HURRICANE PARTY

AKRON SERIES IN POETRY

Akron Series in Poetry
Mary Biddinger, Editor

Alison Pelegrin, *Hurricane Party*
Matthew Guenette, *American Busboy*
Joshua Harmon, *Le Spleen de Poughkeepsie*
David Dodd Lee, *Orphan, Indiana*
Sarah Perrier, *Nothing Fatal*
Oliver de la Paz, *Requiem for the Orchard*
Rachel Dilworth, *The Wild Rose Asylum*
John Minczeski, *A Letter to Serafin*
John Gallaher, *Map of the Folded World*
Heather Derr-Smith, *The Bride Minaret*
William Greenway, *Everywhere at Once*
Brian Brodeur, *Other Latitudes*
Jeff Gundy, *Spoken among the Trees*
Alison Pelegrin, *Big Muddy River of Stars*
Roger Mitchell, *Half/Mask*
Ashley Capps, *Mistaking the Sea for Green Fields*
Beckian Fritz Goldberg, *The Book of Accident*
Clare Rossini, *Lingo*
Vern Rutsala, *How We Spent Our Time*
Kurt Brown, Meg Kearney, Donna Reis, Estha Weiner, eds.,
Blues for Bill: A Tribute to William Matthews
Sharmila Voorakkara, *Fire Wheel*
Dennis Hinrichsen, *Cage of Water*
Lynn Powell, *The Zones of Paradise*

Titles published since 2003.
For a complete listing of titles published in the series, go to www.uakron.edu/uapress/poetry

ALISON PELEGRIN

HURRICANE PARTY

The University of Akron Press
Akron, Ohio

16 15 14 13 12 5 4 3 2 1

LIBRARY OF CONGRESS CATALOGING-IN-PUBLICATION DATA

Pelegrin, Alison. Hurricane party / Alison Pelegrin. p. cm.—(Akron series in poetry) ISBN 978–1-935603–08–5 (cloth : alk. paper)—ISBN 978–1-935603–09–2 (pbk. : alk. paper) I. Title. PS3566.E363H87 2011 811.'54—dc22 2011008198

The paper used in this publication meets the minimum requirements of ANSI/NISO Z39.48–1992 (Permanence of Paper). ∞

Cover: *Water Sky*, by Damara Kaminecki, copyright © 2008. Used with permission. Cover design: Amy Freels

Hurricane Party was designed and typeset in Minion, with Futura display, by Amy Freels and Zac Bettendorf. *Hurricane Party* was printed on sixty-pound natural and bound by BookMasters of Ashland, Ohio.

ACKNOWLEDGMENTS

Some of the poems in this collection first appeared in other publications: "Katrina Scribendi" in *32 Poems;* "Hurricane Party," "Blue Balls," "River of Voices," and "The Family Jewels" in *Barn Owl Review;* "Self-Portrait in a Tourist's Snapshots" in *Blackbird;* "Funky from Now On" in *Brilliant Corners;* "Love Poem with Schooner and Ruins" in *Cave Wall;* "Where Y'at" and "Praying with Strangers" in *Copper Nickel;* "Dispatch to Runaway the Younger" and "Little Song for Kimberly" in *Country Dog Review;* "Our Lady of Prompt Succor" in *Crab Creek Review;* "Shadow Ode," "Raw Oysters with my Rock Star Husband," "Foosball, Shania, and Thou," and "Joy Ride on the Gretna Ferry" in *Diode*; "Helicopter Hands" in *Ducts.org;* "Stupid Praise" in *Image;* "A Brief History of My Life" and "50-cent Words" in *The Journal;* "The Last Holdout" in *Linebreak;* "Ode to Things" in *New Plains Review;* "Pit Bull Pastoral" in *The Normal School;* "Invitation to the Gretna Royals" in *Oxford American;* "The Day the Music Stopped" in *Measure;* "Tubing on the Bogue Chitto" in *The Pinch*; "Tabasco in Space" in *Ploughshares;* "Louisiana," and "Ode to Booze" in *River Styx;* "Something in the Water" in *The Rumpus;* "Blessings for a Nemesis" in *Southern Humanities Review*; "Daughter of the Confederacy" in *Southern Women's Review;* "The Creeps" in *Southern Poetry Review;* "Cumpleaños" and "Louisiana Crude" in *Sou'wester;* "Mid-City Tours" in *Sugar House Review;* "Bestiary of the Bayou State" in *Valparaiso Poetry Review.*

I want to offer a sincere thank you to the people behind the scenes who offered support. The generosity of the National Endowment for the Arts and sabbatical leave from Southeastern Louisiana University helped me to begin these poems. Funding from the Dorothy Sargent Rosenberg Memorial Fund and the encouragement of journal editors and poet friends, especially Sandy Longhorn, helped along the way. The University of Akron Press has been wonderful to work with (again). Special thanks to Amy Freels for her flourishes. My editor Mary Biddinger has cheered me from the beginning—I am lucky to have her in my corner.

Thanks to my family, especially my mom.

Hubby Bryan Davidson—I can't do it without you.

ART WORKS.
arts.gov

for Ben & Sam

Contents

River of Voices 3
Louisiana 4
A Brief History of My Life 6
The Creeps 7
Mid-City Tours 9
Self-Portrait in a Tourist's Snapshots 10
Burying the Hatchet 11
Joy Ride on the Gretna Ferry 12
Daughter of the Confederacy 14
The Last Holdout 16
Little Song for Kimberly 17
Where Y'at 18
Ode to Things 19
Dispatch to Runaway the Younger 21
Cumpleaños 22

The Family Jewels 25
Our Lady of Prompt Succor 26
Funky from Now on 27
Ode to Booze 28
The N-Word 30
Bestiary of the Bayou State 31
Foosball, Shania, and Thou 33
Blue Balls 34
Tubing on the Bogue Chitto 35
Pit Bull Pastoral 36
Hangman 37
Blessings for a Nemesis 38
Ode to the Pelican 39
Raw Oysters with My Rock Star Husband 40

Hurricane Party 43
Praying with Strangers 45
The Day the Music Stopped 46
50-cent Words 47
Something in the Water 49
Shadow Ode 50
What I Did on My Summer Vacation 51
Louisiana Crude 53
Love Poem with Schooner and Ruins 54
Helicopter Hands 55
Katrina Scribendi 56
Stupid Praise 57
Invitation to the Gretna Royals 58
Tabasco in Space 59

Notes 63

River of Voices

I have this inarticulate theory of being wronged.
I can't shut up about it. I'm hooked on Katrina,
my worst luck (and I was lucky!) doling out
sucker punches, ulcers, and suspect fruit,
and who can make peace with bloody kisses?
There should be a twelve-step group, a safe house
FEMA trailer reachable by sea legs up the porch.
Once inside you'd gather around the card table,
light hurricane candles, and mumble the Serenity Prayer.
Starting over should be so easy. One day
at a time you wake and reenter a world
where everybody has flood stories and a Sheetrock cough.
The stories hum in my mind like bees in the wall—
river of voices rising to the watermark of what I choose
to remember, to breathe away from myself in one
long anonymous ode to mercy and decay.
Oh happy day, when it became okay to laugh!
Twinkle lights on the trash heap of soured clothes.
Our first practical joke, our first *faux pas* in months,
involving citrus from a neighbor's tree that stood weeks
in flood waters, feigned death, but come spring
flourished with fruit. Post-Katrina etiquette
is so confusing! Is it okay to take the oranges that fall,
and if it is okay to take, is it okay to eat the flood-
nourished fruit, and if one is unsure, is it okay
to pass the first taste off to an unsuspecting relative,
and once we see no harm is done, how long
are we allowed to laugh? A bystander would think
we took this on for fun, this reunion
of family at the table long after the meal
is cleared, telling our stories, which are one
story, the same story over and again,
only sometimes a few words added or missing,
story which, despite its heartbreak and body count
has always been about rebirth.

Louisiana

“The state with the prettiest name,”
and with parishes: Evangeline, Rapides, Avoyelles,
Tangipahoa, which in Choctaw means “corncob people.”
Fantastical sinking state, of a boot the heel-toe-heel
invisible, one football field a day drowned
to sop the Mississippi’s mighty slop.
(As pretty names go, in second place.)
I-will-not-speak-French-in-the-schoolyard state.
State snake-in-the-mailbox, and cane fields
lined with rails and jails, and two-seater churches.
Throw me something, mister state. Coonass central,
but don’t you say it. And don’t spell Cajun with a K.
Our postcard more faux than the jackalope:
alligator chomping on a wet-T hottie’s rump.
There hasn’t been a gator death in years,
but our license plates speak the truth—
Sportsman’s Paradise—for noodlers, nutria trappers,
boar wrestlers, ruff riders on land and at sea.
Frequent in this land are freak show fishing holes
where monster catfish breach for kibbles.
(No scales, you know. And those barbs sting.)
What’s not sinking here leans. Power lines
sag like jump ropes. Porches slope.
Unless nailed down, a rocking chair will drift
in the blue roof state. Katrina-rigged,
stagnant-minded state, with horns locked
in hoop skirt times where—look away, kudzu!—
where the rebel flag’s a favorite window dressing
and tattoo. Stomping ground of Civil War
rememberers, their gray coats muddying
the healing greens of Jean Lafitte.
State of roughneck uncles missing fingers,
their wedding bands on stubs instead.

Every other man a *parrain,* or a convict
on work release, like the mower who steered
his tractor clear of purple highway flowers.
Can he read? Does he know someone wrote back?
One word spray painted on the overpass—*Thanx.*

A Brief History of My Life

Call it a crap shoot or ambrosial luck,
    a Hail Mary pass through galaxies of pink—
somehow I crash landed in my Gretna cradle
    during the disco era, my back-of-the-house people
with their gap teeth looking down, singing
    the Bee Gees, making Big Bird on the birthday cake
eat a fried shrimp, toke a cigarillo. Oh, shenanigans
    and snapshots too stupid to label—picnic tables,
tailgating in the driveway, its ruts filled with blue rocks
    from the fish tank. Cousins cooling off in jail
for slurred words or their general overexuberance.
    Reformed through craft therapy, the Twelve Steps,
and the healing touch of duck named Pluto,
    the ex-cop my uncle served time in Angola
for masterminding a den of cop thieves.
    He made amends by rebuilding my first car,
a 1978 Mercury Comet, aka *La Tortuga.*
    That was in high school. Then for a decade
I ignored the red flags of blessings and luck.
    A made-for-TV life. A honky tonk cliché.
You can take the girl out of Gretna, but never Gretna
    out of the girl—mother's prophecy haunting me
more accurate than DNA. How true in my stormy age
    of clove cigarettes and escape. My crossed eyes
bored by everything—I thought it made me wise.
    I've gone soft. It only took the church to rid me
of malaise, healer Pat's anointing with a touch of oil.
    Wait till you hear what she said—*Get the devil*
behind you, child, and write the poems.

The Creeps

For starters, wrinkled hands, the veins
that show, elbow skin sagging
over table's edge, snakes in my shoes,

the babysitter's retarded brother watching
while she rinsed my hair. Blindness,
especially Granny's—her cloudy blues,

her hibiscus slip covers specked with crumbs
because when she swept, she swept nothing,
or she swept roaches thinking they were raisins.

Prophesies, eye teeth, toy breeds,
being cut on, the wrong limb removed,
and that's just me. Among my kind,

sirens in the heart at the hint of blood,
of the hospital, or its white-coated troops,
ever since Grandpa Thompson in his youth

so panicked in the baby ward he split
and never met his twin spawn, Earl
and Pearl, until they came home,

natural-born wincers the pair of them.
Home sweet home, no haven
if you spook easily and look for signs,

jumpy in broad day thanks to thigh-highs
in the tub drip-drying like disembodied
line dancers, or the ghosts of pudgy legs.

All my life, cool air through the door
and their coven of voices calling out bets
on Up and Down the River. Almost at ease

but for their imperfections—the toupees,
the meaty moles, the yellow teeth clacking,
constant metronomes of chatter.

How they cackled about the wall mount,
a moose whose ham, they swore, peekabooed
in the guest bedroom. Well, hear me testify.
I searched Nanny's closet, split the coats in half—nothing.

Mid-City Tours

Marching band in the street, flock
of green parrots wild in the palm trees' fruit,
and only my son looks up, double honks
a bird call on his plastic trumpet.
A tour guide, whose job it was to point,
my father could have moved the crowd
to notice. He befriended random people,
even at red lights where he'd roll down
the window to chitchat and give a peace sign
to jaywalkers who ignored him.
In the hatchback on the way home
after a day of city tours, his hand gestured
out of habit to Bayou St. John, called
by the Indians *Tchoupic* for its muddy water.
No such thing as a day of rest—
we ghost-hunted after the good luck of rain,
listening for whispers in cemeteries
and elsewhere, and it's true that steam rising
from the streets really does seem to call
your name. Bring-your-daughter-to-work day,
this time a plantation tour, he used
his hobo charm on cooks
with white skin and period dress.
They heaped us with loaves of bread,
bounty enough to share, and so
we took the ground streets home—
Canal Street to Carrollton, our escort
a drum line of grit and dragged feet.

Self-Portrait in a Tourist's Snapshots

Tourist, in a white carriage by a donkey
pulled backwards, is that what you call
the Big Easy life? Look at you—

feather boa bold at the piano bar,
bugging your waiter for the same old songs.

I've been there, at the fountain, holding court
with a tambourine and a shot glass of limes.

Mira! My gringa foot inside the powwow circle.

Blur of red sequins, red carnival mask,
pencil beard smeared—can't always tell
which devil I am, which baby doll,

what the glitter letters on umbrellas spell
when the divas line up in order of height.

At the second line parade, I'm one step
closer than you to the fanned-out ostrich plumes
and orange, thrown-down tuxedo jackets.

Sammy, my youngest, rides my shoulders.
We're in the gig. Tuba boss blows back at us.
The gravediggers shovel and sing.

Do me a favor—right the plastic flowers
in the vase before you start
a charcoal rubbing of my people's names and dates.

When you look down from the charter bus window
like a politician on a goodwill tour,
I'm drinking hose water

against a backdrop of pink insulation thistles.

Burying the Hatchet

Robber barons of the coffers of joy, zealots
of good times squandered on a lark of mean.
Beware the rage that dogs you to the grave.

The schism in the House of P broke out
fifty-something years ago. In Thibodeaux.
Good times squandered on a lark of mean.

The Mason-Dixon drawn inside our name.
Two *l*'s to one. Don't know exactly why.
Fifty-something years ago. In Thibodeaux,

everywhere, my name misspelled on signs.
Just passing through, my hackles rise.
Two *l*'s, not one—don't know exactly why.

Pellegrin Homebuilders. Pellegrin Marine.
Lies! No matter how they spell the name
just passing through, my hackles rise.

Once a decade, when snow falls in the swamp,
we reach across parish lines, kiss and make up.
Yeah, right. No matter how you spell your name,
beware the rage that dogs you to the grave.

Joy Ride on the Gretna Ferry

In summer we are all alike—
storm-wary and reckless for a breeze.

Bikes and cars on the lower deck, pedestrians above.

A procession of the good people of my world,
murder capital of the world.

Mismatched office ladies who will scatter
into the mirrored office buildings downtown,
waiters trailing apron strings, street dancers
stomping bottle cap taps in their shoes.

My sons follow suit, beg me down to the lower deck,
and so we go, and they go straight to the edge.

They could fall in. They could chip a tooth,
but rather they offer gum wrappers
from the bottom of my purse to the water, to the wind.

Dizzy when the boat moves—looking forward,
pulled back to school days I made this trip with my mother
not for a joy ride, but because we missed the bus.

She'd get us as far as Jackson Avenue then transfer
and leave me as ward of a bus driver who could not care less.

I smeared my name, circled it with a heart
in the grease spot on the window, mistrustful of street signs
and others' directions, and thus eternally disoriented
by landmarks creeping up over the wrong shoulder.

The levees rimming the Mississippi hide everything—
of churches, only the steeples remain.

City of crosses and skulls, of teddy bears and bouquets
along fences to remind that some have fallen, some floated away.

I think I hear cathedral bells, or sirens, or else my sons
in their musical shoes. Life jackets everywhere,
a bright orange wall of bricks.

Daughter of the Confederacy

Down here, news travels slow. Fathers and sons,
they fall and rise, they raise the Southern Cross,
they pilgrimage to battlefields in Vicksburg,
Richmond, and swing the metal detector
with prayers for a crop of stunted bullets.

Photo op all through childhood: Me and my brother
beside Fort Jackson's black-washed cannon
in order of height. Picnic and relic hunting after.

We found skipping stones, nothing more,
but kept the faith, believed ourselves transformed
by a stroll through damp brick caves.
Chilled ankles while we stooped
for a cannon's view of the river's curves—
we thought it was a dead man's breath.

Ancestor worship. One foot in the past.
In Baton Rouge, retirees underfoot
at the front desk of the special collections library
where I fetched their maps, disarmed them
of contraband ink pens and coffee thermoses.

Any visitor could be a vandal with a vat of paint,
and the curators so mistrusted enthusiasm
I crept by, traitor with a whitewash heart
set against my name written in gray
in the roster of Union and Confederate dead.

Reckless before I quit. Sloppy, bored, irreverent,
tempted to alter the files, the endless files
in rows like headstones in Arlington cemetery.
Hardly wrong when no one knows to come looking,
and if a scholar wastes her footnote summer, so what?

The whispers hounding me down the halls—
at first I chalked it up to white guilt, or a Yankee ghost
showering dust on the displays, karma hounding me
for all those school trips to the Confederate Museum

where I marveled at a guide detailing hacksaw amputation,
Confederate bills stamped with cotton bales,
and what seemed ladies' hats behind the glass. . . .
Did they have shrunken heads?

The whispers came from preservationists,
idolaters of factoids and fading paint,
plotting how best to preserve portraits
of Southern generals. Their battle plan?
When no one is looking, flip them nose-to-the-wall.

I know about their reenactments and period falconry,
the Farbys and thread counters, buffs
groomed with pockmarks and period grimaces,
the beards in shaded portraits their hand mirrors.

Perhaps you have seen them at close of day—
the regiments, moth-bitten, gray,
that slouch towards a battle lost long ago,
bottlenecking all the back roads.
I wait them out at the gas station
that sells moonshine and meat pies.

Across the street, reenactment brides.
In a circle they pray—thanks be given—
again their rebels rise up from the dust,
stinking of sweat and antique wool.
They call themselves the new endangered species
and walk among us resurrecting history.

The Last Holdout

I half expected to find your name, Dad, the obit
telling, like so many others, of wild times
and remains released from St. Gabriel's morgue
three months after the flood, zipped in black,
the yellow teeth alone making sense. Ever since
you dove from iron steps into the condo pool
during a pre-landfall lightning storm,
we've bet on you kicking it by hurricane.

I wish you'd come back and play the holdout
that you are—one last season of mojitos
and gold medallions. Just like before—
ignore our pleas, ignore the mayor's call,
and sit tight with your stash of fruit cocktail
while your sisters twist their rosaries in Monroe.

I'll take anything but the call that came
in the middle of the night—death's understudy,
death's friend-of-a-friend—and the chaos
of dressing in yesterday's clothes, more of us
crammed in the Cadillac than clowns
in a circus wagon. Then the waiting,
our scarlet frowns horseshoes aiming south,
Uncle Al jump-starting the vigil when we dozed
by jerking your brain-dead bed and shouting,
It's a miracle! He moved, but you were unchanged.
Your eyes roamed everywhere but to our faces.

At least you'll never know how we made out
or that they offer devastation tours of the Ninth Ward—
truck on roof, barge on car and car, shotgun house
shifted two blocks from where its pilings stand.
You'd never lead a tour headed that way,
like me holding sacred what the flood line
underscores, grim chorus of painted words.

Little Song for Kimberly

Child, don't bother tracking down your kin.
Keep Out. Police line—can't come in. Though I guess
You'll wonder why you're mean like a Marine,
Where you got them smarts. Blame it on us—
Olympic liars, aka your mama's side.
We never knew there was a you, I swear.
And once we did, Amanda said you died,
Sent us hunting for your cremains everywhere.
The ones who have you now can't be so bad.
I bet you never toddle in the dirt
With a filthy face and hands. When you get mad,
Don't wish for us. What hurts won't always hurt.
Your mother knew she couldn't do no better.
She's dead. She died young. You look just like her.

Where Y'at

Now I will sing the Louisiana drawl.
For to me it is a joyful noise, more better than the blues or funk
or Dixieland jazz.
For this is the language of kings, like my grandfather Royal, and it holds
more music than newscaster-speak.
For my mama-n-them, when they angry they drawl it best.
To find out, just laugh when they say "shrimps."

For I was brought up right, and I know things.
Like, you're supposed to feed me before starting in with questions.
For I can stump the sphinx who riddles, "Who's your mama, are you
Catholic, and can you make a roux?'
For I will tell, but first I want a Creole tomato from Plaquemines Parish.
For in taste they are divine, being sometimes grown in the shade of
pecan trees.

For true, at the lunch counter I love a long wait just to be near the
unspellable speak of the cooks.
For you would have to hear it to believe.
For God has sent this waitress to the table to shower me with *Have a
blessed day.*
For all the children at Mandina's feel it when our hands halo above their
heads but never alight.

For when the city sleeps I have caught myself listening in on FEMA trailers.
For, like I said, when they angry they drawl it best.
For some can rock the trailer with their curses.

For sometimes I will scoot through a crowd and touch everyone I pass,
A secret dance I come up with the night Tuba Fats (sign of the cross, may
he rest in peace) saw me from the stage.
For he must have meant me when he hollered, "Can I get an Amen, sister?"

For everyone looked my way, and I told him, "Yeah, you rite!"
My voice one voice in the gospel choir.

Ode to Things

Dumpsters of things,
shiny baubles of the earth,
things we collect
then discard or forget—
paperclips, state capitol
teaspoons, marbles,
baby food jars
with buttons inside.
Avalanche of artwork—
every doodle a keeper
at first, Sam's circus
tents more like wild
wild west volcanoes
spewing clowns. Bookmarks,
banana phones, spatulas,
shuttlecocks, goggles,
Pink Pearl erasers,
my dead father's clothes,
his dancing shoes,
and in a landfill
between here and Texas,
cousin Amanda's
ballerina jewelry box
bereft of corsages,
of brass rings that rash
fat fingers green.
Endless inventory,
pharaoh's tomb
crowded with vessels,
the jackal god's
hieroglyphic rant
on the wall.
Stolen things, seashell
barrette I lifted

in Ft. Lauderdale,
bicycles, lawnmower
wheeled out of the garage
in winter, while the grass
slept. Nobody noticed,
which reminds me
of the time I ran away—
took Sock Monkey
around the block to mope
beneath a willow tree.
Father is gone, and,
no pharaoh,
his things remain.
We boxed his clothes
for Goodwill, and now
on park benches
everywhere other pawpaws
feed pigeons, reach
for mints in the pockets
of *his* plaid shirts.
Even the word "thing,"
world's vaguest, most
versatile place holder.
There are some things
you'll never understand.
Bring me that thing
over there—no, not
that—the gizmo
with Day of the Dead beadwork.
Doodad from Oaxaca
beside the *TV Guide*.
There, on the nightstand,
right by your hand.

Dispatch to Runaway the Younger

In snapshots, even, reaching for the smokes, that's them.
Five generations, a huddle of hard times—Granny,
Hip, Guy, your mother Chris and baby you,
center of the crèche, in my old christening dress.
This picture is the only proof that in the beginning
they did right by you. All your hair ribbons,
report cards—saved. Since then you've been dragged,
a weapon in divorce, to so many trailer parks
we let it slide and just catch up at funerals.

The last send-off—two, three years ago—was Grandma.
Out of nowhere, cousin, you arrived via cab,
comrade in tow, but not your phantom daughter.
You married? No. Any pictures? No. Does she,
this Kimberly, favor us? No answer. We wonder,
was she ever born? Did the state (which one?) step in?
When you called to say the girl was dead, so what?
She could have been anything. Or nothing. I never believed.

There will always be girls like you, faking disabilities
for pills, cloudy-minded, on extended stay in motels stocked
with strange bedfellows, hitching rides on big rigs
underlit by neon lines and safe-seeming only because
their reflectors spell out crosses and doves. Girls who depend
on Samaritan truckers tag-teaming by code name on the CB,
ferrying hatchbacks into truck stops, powered by fumes.

A semi of merci led your mother to Amarillo.
All her hounding led her to your hospice bed where
lots of answers, with you, cousin, are doomed to fade.
This we deserve. This crossroads, what led us here, I'm not so sure.
You're out of it, ripping at the sheets, the nurses' touch,
arguing with us or the angels on the ceiling. You babble on,
crying. Please, Jesus, let that be the morphine talking.

Cumpleaños

When was it born in me—little itch of scorn
for my people, with unexpected pride mixed in?
We weren't white trash, but on the backslide down
from working class to unemployed to drunk.
My uncles at the Tarpon Rodeo is my guess,
though it could have been before
that afternoon they lifted me from a nap
to witness their deep sea haul—
a hammerhead shark, taller than the boat—
hoisted above them on the dock. In every picture
of that day a different man's eyes are closed,
and then there's me, little miss too-good-for-this,
fake smiling like a pageant queen.
Their lady boat, *The Stripper*, is long gone,
but that day they were all smiles,
indulging me with anything I hinted at,
including Dos Gringos, where the waitresses
made like it was my birthday with a serenade
from under the brims of their sombreros.
After a spit bath and a change of shirts
in the car, my three uncles squeezed
themselves into one side of a booth,
believing that gesture to be crown jewel
of the best day of my life. Maybe it was.
Good old days—I keep a list in secret,
list I hope to make sense of later—
every costume, every drop of blood,
and on feast days the ice chest trembling with fish.

The Family Jewels

Love me, love me not. I don't hate the South.
Or maybe I do. I hate fiction writers spewing
Faulkner's rules at me—*a writer without a bottle*
of whiskey is like a chicken without a goddamn head.
I learned that babysitting—snuck bourbon
in a Dixie cup then diluted the bottle down to rainwater
and compared my answers with theirs in a stack
of Playboy quizzes, vowing to catch up
by flashing a cab driver, answering the door naked.
Church of Faulkner fiction class in grad school,
we went back and forth: the museum's on fire,
and it's up to you to choose between a Vermeer
and a random grandmother—you can only save one.
We all know what Faulkner said—
"Ode on a Grecian Urn" is worth any number of old ladies.
I want to agree. As a poet I maybe should,
but I think of Emily Dickinson behind a screen
writing, all cameo and concentration, teaching,
I think, that it's the act, not artifact. I'm not in love
with Keats' Ode—"To Autumn" is better, but even *mists*
of mellow fruitfulness elicits a so what
when I think of my mother—a little old lady now,
with her netti pot and tissues up the sleeve. In her will,
it says for me to pull the plug and bury her cheap,
instructions left in triplicate with Aunt Joan, the lawyer,
and in a box of rhinestones hogtied with bungee cords
and labeled, as a joke on thieves, The Family Jewels.

Our Lady of Prompt Succor

Protect us from hurricanes and floods

Not Catholic but *almost,* my middle name
Marie, iambic you. I knelt on rice
in Catholic schools, cropped the Our Father,
but you never wept tears of oil for me,
just stared off, disappointed, into space.
Mother Mary, in resin in our senior rings,
hitching a ride wherever our hands dared travel.
Oh, virginity!—a sin even to think it—me, Mary,
and a Brother Martin boy in the backseat
making our own weather—forecast fog,
and your tears the rain rising as steam from the street.
They say your heart bleeds for the Crescent City,
in strange ways upending fate—the fire of 1812
miraculously snuffed at the convent steps,
dozens of hurricanes by your devoted prayed away.
Even when levees buckle and the rogue winds
devastate, your effigies remain mostly upright
in a thousand gardens, apparitions of lichens and white.
There are other hurricane saints, you know.
The gilded ones, Saint Hildegard of Hungary
and Gregory the Wonderworker, not to mention
God's people on the ground: the Cajun boat brigade,
food looters, helicopter pilots, deputized nurses
sleeping in shifts in the hospital chapel.
You were there in the corner looking spent,
dusty silk flowers at your feet, like a beautified
Sister Hillary, our band camp chaperone. Has she
crossed over, her man shoes and mustache gone
to ash? Sister Mary Hillary up and down the hallway
with a flashlight, plagued by our boy talk,
her lullaby the Latin Mass. She prayed for us, you gave
your answer—infinity of pencil leads, the rain.

Funky from Now on

Normally I wouldn't pay the fortune teller any mind,
but that night I did—I followed the light,
only it wasn't The Light, it was the Rebirth Brass Band
funking it up under a white tent at Voodoo Fest.
So many gold teeth sparkling, some of them
accented with diamonique, others
with cutouts of a half-moon, say,
or a creature of the zodiac.
Along with the smiles shined the tuba bell,
playing the world so that the onlookers
hung there, dummy quotes in a fun house
of movers and shakers. No room for background noise,
and so loud my heart skipped a beat—rebirth?
Ulcer? Cardiac arrest? Next thing I know,
I'm following the lead of Lady Tambourine,
second lining where she does, her pink falsetto heels
sinking into the grass, my hips bumping
the folding chairs out of their cornrows.
The song is teasing, but I do, I do believe
I could be a Rebirth Brother. So they will know
that I'm for real, I put my feelers out,
and I must have sung it with them a thousand times,
Everything I do gonna be funky from now on.

Ode to Booze

At least
you give me things
to write about.
I am the tooth fairy,
and I am drunk,
my lawn chair aimed
in the wrong direction
on the night
of the red eclipse.
At sixteen, missing you,
I stole or talked up guys
in painters' clothes
outside the liquor store.
They'd have bought
anything. I asked for
Mad Dog 20/20.
Grape. It's you
and me, booze.
Vino, vodka breath,
little beers for when I fish,
backwash in the bottle
and we two awake
watching reruns
of *Three's Company.*
Oh, how I love
to revisit the décor
of my childhood.
Macrame! and mirrors!
I'm past the age
of my father
when he dried out
for good, what they call
a "high bottom." All
it took was handcuffs

and a scuffle
at the gas station.
One night in jail
and *voilà*—he's walking
the walk. Serenity this,
serenity that. Disloyal
me shrugs it off.
My heart's needle
pulls south. Misfits
I have known—
addicts, and broads,
roughneck brothers
hogging the floor
in AA meetings,
and me a retread
before I was twenty.
I never understood
their two weeks
on, two off, until I was
sober seven years,
with the tattoos
to prove it. No
troubles, no reason
but money in my pocket,
and (oh, no,
here we go
again), I let
the counter tick
back to zero.

The N-Word

I have cringed when I have heard—how many times?—
my people pull the trigger on the n-word.
Interjection most foul, splinter, Band-Aid yanked
without warning by the school nurse, her skin
the color of a tongue depressor. Reflex
at the altar with the host in the mouth
placed there always by a wrinkled white hand.
I took to bed without supper once—on my birthday—
locked down in my room for *not* repeating It
on command. The life of a saint if not for pride.
Pride and the wish that I could mutter
one of its high octane understudies, in a whisper,
to make my people proud. My people, coonass proud,
coonass a slur condemned by linguists
as meaning nothing, less than nothing, really,
because they take it to mean "less than black."
Look at them—the whole back row at church.
Less than black, and less than French, their *jolie*
Cajun words shamed out of them by nuns,
so that what's left is worn thin like Sunday shoes
passed down a ladder of sisters. Wicked trochee.
Crippled heartbeat. Wince every step of the walk.

Bestiary of the Bayou State

Armadillos, unlucky under wheels, linger
with their stench on Million Dollar Road.
Blind nearly, born in sets of four, they jump UP
when alarmed instead of playing possum. My
cat kills one of those a night. At least I think
she's the one that drops them—sleeping?
dead?—on a newspaper pillow at dawn.
Good girl, mama kitty, wildebeest, rabbit
eater, cougarlike and almost tame.
She suffers kindness after she's rolled in
fresh kill. Chains of ants pour from the eyes of
field mice, moles, and featherless birds.
Gators everywhere, and in everything—
from blood sausage to cowboy boots.
Hunting them, you gaff first, then shoot, or else
they'll sink. Chicken necks or tripe for bait. An
invite of mini-marshmallows draws them
closer to the boat. Sometimes too close—
just last summer one took a boy's arm.
He survived. Not so for "Big Joe."
Killer bees, honey bees, swarm of bees in my hair,
and me howling through the bayou
like a *loup garou* with a mouthful of baby shoes.
Many arrowheads and blades to nick the garfish.
Mullet, trash fish, bottom feeders triple jumping
on the Tickfaw River's houseboat side.
Nobody but the down-and-outs even bother,
the bridge-dwellers, hunger's hounds, their bicycles
overloaded with nets and mildewed umbrellas.
How come this sterile outline on the state flag,
Pelican? They've made you over, more mascot than
mother love. No self-let blood to feed the
quints, no crash dives near the Causeway where martins
swarm at dusk—I hit three with the car one trip.
Red and yellow, friendly fellow—or is it red and yellow,

kill a fellow? Jack? Which snake has poisonous
stripes? This is how I know poetry
can't save me. Guaranteed I'll handle the
toxic snake, as though for me they'd be charmed,
as though from my acreage alone
undergrowth would be purged of insect dangers
and the copperhead's paper skin. Drive slow while
vultures lift off from their red velvet road kill.
Nothing wasted, nothing left behind. Well, almost.
Woodpeckers, we spared the half-dead tree; you split it
Like a lightning strike. We hold our voices down, O
xylophone of unseen birds—ruddy ducks randomly
off cue, battle hymn of hawks and crows.
You can hear carpenter bees drilling the porch swing.
See their sawdust rain? Dizzying—a
zillion devil crickets dead at the creek bed—
down payment for the few that wobble onward.

Foosball, Shania, and Thou

Honey, call me bear and I'll climb you
in the shelter of the walking oak, booze you
with blueberry wine stewed summer-long
in the crawl space beneath the porch.
Hand fishing summer, summer of perfecting
carnival strength so to win a monster teddy
at the fair. Stalled van with the sofa seats,
bells and blue glass chimes in the trees—please.
Sit by me on a milk crate bench
like at the drive-in, our movie the moon
shrouded in fog, or grackles that trespass
autumn grasses like a scene from a Chinatown fan.
My old life torched in the burn pile, baby,
that's how much I'll mend my ways.
Them hawks above the stinking ditch,
stray dragging muddy teats—safe.
I don't shoot because of you. Look at me—
off my game, writing a poem a day. I won't ask
anymore for you to scout while I drag race.

Blue Balls

With Bumper Nutz for duallies and monster trucks,
who needs fuzzy dice or a dashboard Jesus?
I prefer them life-size with baby names—tenders,
or jewels—something to cradle and protect,
not sandbags dragging from Humvee convoys
in Afghanistan. A gag gift, the new pet rock—
choco balls, bubble gum and lime, red hot
Tabasco balls with popping veins. Camo balls
for four wheelers, and for breast men, awareness
pinkies like cow bells to and fro from tow hitches
in the Walmart parking lot. A desire rises
in me—I want to get crafty, to get dirty
on my knees, on my back, underneath,
just like in high school, but with candle wax
and a glue gun, spangle them with glitter and sequins
and *voilà*! Liberace balls dragging across speed bumps
leaving, instead of skid marks, sparkle in their wake.
I feel so bad for you, Big Boys, hung with twin
Christmas hams—those things look like they hurt.
I used to have a rabbit's foot key chain I rubbed
for luck; now there are Bitty Balls, pocket nutz
swinging from the ignition, their whisper
of a touch against my knee on all my travels.
Is this what it's like to be a man? Is this
what inspires one to raise the question on a T-shirt,
Do you want to ride my fat boys? I'll bet
you say that to all the girls, to the Hooters girls
in gravel tickling your pick up's manly flesh.
Country boy, in blue jeans, straddling the blue balls
chained to your truck—what's wrong with this picture?
Hint hint—it's not *your* package, a sky-blue rabbit's foot
bulging through your Wranglers—but the other—
that-which-must-be cock-socked, tucked away on first dates
and church picnics—disco electric, neon hernia,
baby daddy, ball and chain, blue bird of happiness balls.

Tubing on the Bogue Chitto

I don't know my snakes—they all seem
poisonous—and here, the road in
is the road out, a copperhead coiled on a rock.
Amber dust coats the car like powder
from a moth's wings. The worst sunburn
of my life is on the way. I can feel it. Red skin,
redneck river at the dirt road's end. River
of ghosts, river of garbage, of beer cans
in wire baskets, river where no ass is too fat
for rebel flag boxer shorts. River reminding
me that in a way, the South did win,
at least for show. This was Choctaw land—
these brown silk waters and flea-bitten sands.
What have I done in bringing my sons here,
dropped by a school bus hours upstream?
I skipped church for this—sensible,
civilized church—only to be eclipsed
by a fundamentalist youth group
with a sermon on their floating radio.
I am afraid we won't get out,
and my husband has rock band hair.
I'm on high alert, each son's inner tube
tied with twine to mine. I feel like crying.
I shut my mouth at the sound of guns
and paddle with my hands through
the southern wilds. A swamp gas smell
ruins our picnic lunch. We toss hot dogs
to a coon hound abandoned
on the bank, and he howls
like the ghost of something that belongs.

Pit Bull Pastoral

Follow the ditches where minnows flinch
from litter and spit, follow the fencing's lead
and one or other clam shell road will weave
past a fighting ring, where baseball bats
and boot stomps master a dog's muscle mind.
The feed store talk is dogs and glocks.
A flanneled man with red stubble and rebel truck
introduces his Killer Ice—chained
to the trailer hitch—as a message from God.
The Peace Keeper's been listening. He seen
me take my hat off in the storefront church
and alleluia he delivered me this angel
with a devil of a bite. Pit bulls and firewood
for sale in the China South parking lot—
solid black, cayenne, and swamp moss brindle.
Overcrowding shelters, downed on arrival,
pitched in dumpsters, left to bleed out or make
a mad dog dash across the scenic route for shade
beneath a mud-skirted oak. Little black dog,
wagging and wincing, looks like you took a hatchet
to the head—can't you learn? Toothless, ruined,
don't lick my hand—leave it. Shoo. Go on,
surrender your fur to the bird's nest, your hide
to the beaks of crows. If I had a gun I'd fire away
so your soul could give its iron to the clay.

Hangman

Forensics settled on a sneer
for your clay face in the paper asking for a name.

Red clay Choctaw face rebuilt with blue eyes and a snarl,

the gray braid, the speak-no-evil monkey
on your shirt untouched until a four wheeler
and its boy came upon you in spring.

The sheriff's men soon following
staked out a grid and combed the dirt,

uncovered nothing but footprints of their own
and insect hulls in the dust,

nothing but bones and a noose that held
through two hurricanes, the rain dance of decay.

They make you out to be a loner POW/MIA.
No roots, no son or daughter of the earth,

as if you never took a meal in silence,

never handy-manned for room and board,
whittling, singing with the radio on a roll-out bed

where sleep came in jolts, like a fall from a horse.

Blessings for a Nemesis

If you know me, you know who.
A curse word all his own. My nemesis,
my narrow-minded fellow in the grass.

Any promise he makes sounds
like a hiss. I wish him nothing
but the second best. Bargain blessings,

ten for a buck, half-hearted,
like cactus hiccups caught
in my throat. I wish him a wee bit

but not much luck. Jalapeño
jellies in his Easter basket.
The freight train's blessed clockwork:

may every day it stop him first.
Holy bronco, kick his tooth out
at the prison rodeo. Corn maze,

hold him tight till after dark. How much
for an ambush of bats? Each word
from him a tick on my neck.

Shadow fanged, but up front, sweet.
Next time he hunts, may doves
and danger hover out of reach.

Ode to the Pelican

Brown or white, you are the goofiest of birds.
Bird of crash dives and the infinite wattle,
creature most likely to be caricatured

in blown glass, to be carved and clown-painted
in Oaxaca. Albatross of the Gulf, usherer in
of fishing boats, even the psalmist took note:

I am like a pelican of the wilderness. Oh, my soul,
if I could shape shift, it would be you, pelican,
and I'd yawp from your roomiest of throats.

Pelican, Pelegrin: on lazy tongues our names alike.
Wing man of my father as he marathoned across
Lake Pontchartrain with blood in his shoes.

Portrayed prolifically in water colors, but rarely
the topic of a tribal tattoo. Selfless Pelican,
in stained glass second only to the dove,

feeding your trinity of flightless young with shreds
of flesh and sips of your own blood. On the state flag
they've sanitized your cannibal love, Louisiana bird.

What can we do for you, pelican? Oil spoiled,
washing up on toxic beaches. Marbled eggs
unforming while pious, blackened pelicans sit.

I have been faithless. All my life I thought
you were falling—reckless, sprawled like Icarus—
until you surfaced with a fish. Blue-gloved hands

hold you kindly in a tub, flush saline in your eyes,
give your feathers a toothbrush scrub. You fight
by giving up, unwilling or unable to be saved by us.

Raw Oysters with My Rock Star Husband

Last call unless you're with the band,
and since I sometimes write his songs
there's room for me at the bar,
an extra chair for the guitar.

Oil spill on the news, forecast of the flow.
A growing list of fishing places closed.
An oysterman's lament—one last day
in the boat for a goodbye to the Gulf Coast.

Our long goodbye begins with what could be
the last taste for years. We get to work.
One dozen on the half shell with two beers.
We tap the shells together. Cheers.

Hurricane Party

No way in hell the sky would do me wrong.
Even with the weatherman keening
in his yellow slicker, it just doesn't sink in.

Plywood, shrimp boots, sandbags, and booze.
Stuck in line at the hardware store,
pancakes for dinner after schools close early.
Before landfall, before the water comes
and anyone gets hurt,

it's always fun—
chanting the alphabet of named storms
that never harmed besides a muck mosaic
in the streets,

the waterline's footprint
a jagged hem of leaves on the lawn.

Taping the windows, packing
for a midnight exodus, our map
the lava flow of headlights. In the car—
pillows, a coffee can for pee,
and *Michael, row the boat ashore.*

The aggravation makes the worst you've heard
seem not so bad, not even boating
from rooftop to rooftop after Betsy,

or cousin Chancy in the crook of a tree
delivered by a voice speaking out of the light:
Over here—dis child, he cold.

Is it chance, or is God listening when I beg
to be passed over, for someone to take my place
ripping up carpets and breathing the stench
of minnows shriveled on concrete?

Cameron Parish, Yucatan Peninsula,
the whole of Florida, Dominican Republic—
apologies for the times my blessings
have arrived at your expense—

a feast of outage-thawed seafood,
the easy work of peeling tape
from crossed-off windows,

        each pane scraped clean
a day the calendar is giving back.

Praying with Strangers

Wish I could be funny again, like the old me,
    wild child with food and music on the mind,
        because I am worn out with bringing

nothing but needs to the hands of the Lord
    beginning that day I packed the kids in the car
        for a head start against The Hurricane.

Five hours north to the nearest hotel room,
    tears the whole way, like we knew what was coming,
        like we were going to be the ones prying apart

the automatic doors of the Winn Dixie
    to float out unfrozen frozen food.
        Oh, Refugees, oh my stranded sisters

and brothers, we never looked away
    from the television set, our campfire.
        We ate out until the money ran out,

then choked down charity—peanut butter,
    peanut butter, peanut butter, bread.
        I swam in the hotel pool, drawling

reminisces in the company of peers,
    anything to keep my head above water
        in the Bible Belt, where they don't sell beer

on Sundays. Bellyaching, praying with strangers—
    it became my life's work. Didn't want the job,
        but there I was, scratching out words, taking notes,

while my children, their foot soles filthy black,
    played rescue helicopter with their army men
        on the rooftop of the unmade bed.

The Day the Music Stopped

New Orleans, August 29, 2007

No jazz today. Word hurries down Treme,
Down sidewalks and porches—at Armstrong Park
The band set out, and they refuse to play.

No dirge. Rolling slow, the meter maid way,
Pal's Pink Suit Steppers and the Carnival Sharks
Won't jazz today. Word hurries down Treme—

A brass band coming, their groove astray,
Shoe shine, trumpet shine, but no "Closer Walk."
They hold their instruments and do not play.

Last year a mock funeral on this day.
Pine box for Katrina cut loose to the dark,
Then Dixieland jazz in the streets of Treme.

This year we can't make the blues go away.
We've been down so long that music feels like work.
Black sash for the marshal—we can't play.

No jazz today. Word hurries down Treme.
We can't lift our eyes from the watermark.
We're calling, Lord, who hardly ever pray.
The band set out, and they refused to play.

50-cent Words

Dictionary, my lap dog, my little black book,
pick a thumb tab, any letter, and make me
sound smart. As it is, all my tattles
and blathering, all my sound and fury,
I've said zilch. On repeat. Boring the world
with son-of-a-bitches under my breath, *I love you,*
How was your day? Students riding westward, Lethe-bound
with divinest sense, Achaeans, and amphibrachs,
but never oxbow, favonian, sporran. Unless—
Oh, my fatidic soul!—I've murmured in sleep.
Doppelganger! Day and night in mouth and mind.
Anglo Saxon dime-a-dozen drib drab by day,
my forked tongue warbling in dreams
a coloratura: mummer, distelfink, scrimshaw.
Divulged in a whisper wordless words to God,
an inarticulate, cup-runneth-over huzzah
re: my offspring, who live their own language.
Widdershins for how they travel in a whorl,
and sasquatch, between their legs the spot
they squat to wash. First question from my firstborn
to the Magic 8 Ball: Are leprechauns for real?
The icosahedron's sage reply: *It is decidedly so.*
I need some yes/no answers from toilet bowl blue.
I need to calm my nerves atwitter in the dark rehearsing
for the great blackout, the great spelunk, a time
of no words, no trace of me beyond a handprint
on the igneous sky, a smear of cave painter's pigments.
I can see it now, donnybrook among the bards
when they divine the origins of this poem
cat scratched in purple ink on a past due permission slip—
dictionary dip and dive, happenstance and fluke
to the nth degree—they'll revoke my wardrobe
of fear and self-loathing, demand the shibboleth,
at which time, of course, I'll blank. Zounds!
Dear sand canvas, dear message in a bottle,

I'm here on a desert island, coconuts and crabs for friends.
I brought my one book—not the King James,
not the complete plays, just my word bird,
which in a pinch will do as a doorstop, desktop pillow
of despair, fire starter on a dark night of the soul,
but wait—don't even go there.

Something in the Water

Verboten, casual, Katrina-slash-this-is-the-writer's-life poem,
another rule breaker best abandoned. At sea.
Overboard in a wine bottle, in a milk jug float.
The words swim down, and I packrat them all.
Anything else would feel like choosing between my sons
who aren't twins exactly, but enough alike
that their lost teeth, first locks of hair morph
to make a mumbo jumbo in my jewelry box.
The greats have their subjects: love, sex, death.
I have mine: hurricane Katrina, Mardi Gras,
time passes me by with moonscape, owl, and merlot.
Editors pass me by—*Alison, it's hard to get excited*
about Katrina poems as there are so many.
So quick to write me off. They should give thanks.
I could be the quack who sends a soul food
curtail sonnet, or exercise bulimic sister-in-law haiku.
A poem a day about my children, their muddy feet
stuck in boots, rattle of pocket treasures in the dryer.
My darlings, who believe that sea glass could be
Poseidon's knuckle bones, a yarn I came up with
to keep them busy while I draft my Deep South
Canterbury Tales called "Something in the Water."
Up at five to sift the oyster flesh of my brain
for pearls of words. Kids at the door, begging,
May we PLEASE have some breakfast! Yesterday,
mind ablaze, I wrote about this man with a mole
in the center of his forehead that I took
for a bullet hole—he even dragged a zombie leg—
and thought it was a great way to spend my time.

Shadow Ode

June 2010

My boys holler from the Pensacola sands—*I spy*
a dragon, a ninja, a T. rex with a chain saw!
It's not cloud shapes they see, but blobs of oil,
staining tar balls stuck like toothpaste
to their feet. Our first vacation day, I swear,
it rained oil—the van, the floor mats stained.
But we didn't cancel. We arrived, and stayed dry,
and curbed our expectations. We stormed
the beach with inflatable sharks and pirate's life
boogie boards, pioneers taller than our shadows.
We ate the oysters and worried later, keeping watch
on the oil spill live-streaming while engineers
wagered with their snake oil fixes. In the background,
a counter tallying gallons spilled—enough
to fill ten Superdomes and umpteen city blocks.
Another Katrina, a split-screen catastrophe—oil,
and the two-toned grasses of Plaquemines,
or shrimp boats towing boom instead of nets.
The clean-up crews point out dolphins
but aren't allowed to speak to us. At dawn
the sand is sand again. Sand raked with tire tracks.
I keep quiet about what I spy, dead fish and shadows
in the surf, one scoop with the plastic shovel
that reveals oil in layers, like the rings of a tree.
News trucks and camera crews hunt photo ops
up and down the beach. They never leave.
I won't look their way, but another mother runs
after her baby in a ruffled suit kicking toes
in the greasy surf. Their splashing brings to mind
oiled birds thrashing, waiting for relief,
and oiled turtles recuperating at Audubon Zoo.
After Katrina we lined up there on reopening day,
camera ready, and shadowed by the press.
It was the day after Thanksgiving, and me still numb,
grieving like an animal with eyes that looked
nowhere. My boys were toddlers in a wagon then,
clapping their arms open and shut to make alligator shadows.

What I Did on My Summer Vacation

You only thought you knew what we
were up to that summer of working mothers
and a pervert on Carondolet.
I learned I was a Pisces—most evolved
of signs—from the zodiac sex acts
etched in gold on his highball glass.

Did you know the rich kids crowned me
their cause célèbre? If not, I'd still be an outcast
at the country club, no racket
or pleated whites to call my own.

You broke their spell upon arrival
in the orange hatchback
held together with twine. I hated you,
hated our secrets—commodities cheese
by candlelight, the house gone dark
because you were behind with the bills.

I stomped across a sea of party dresses to get to you,
certain those girls could read my walk
and therefore knew I was puberty poor
as well—last to bleed in those days
of shoplifting and rummage sale clothes.

Beer and sex a long way off? Not so.
The perv went up my shirt and down
the other Alison's shorts. He bribed me with
an add-a-pearl necklace courtesy
of a big sis home from Ole Miss.

I was fool enough to wear it, to let them think
I took it, which left me alone
in July to weigh myself ten times a day.

You didn't notice—drugstore perfume,
comb in my back pocket, static on the wrist
transistor radio. You didn't know a thing

until I swiped a roll of dimes—your bus money—
to buy my friends back with a trip to Café du Monde.
More than enough, even for a tip,
which in perfect meanness I divvied out
in the bottom of each water glass.

That waitress with her thick legs and her frown
and hair she cut herself over the sink
was so like you—working for nothing,
two dresses and loafers to wear with all.
As I knew she would, as you would, she took the money
before she ran us off with curses.

Louisiana Crude

May 3, 2010, after thirteen days of oil

Louisiana sweet crude spreads a stain
and roughneck families toss foam wreathes to float.
Eleven missing and we have no names.

From rig to marshland spreads a rainbow sheen.
No prep for this storm but to shore the boat.
Louisiana sweet crude spreads a stain,

but how much, and how long, who knows? Fishing's
closed. The moon is no moon on an asphalt
sea, the stars no stars. Too many birds to name

roost on ruined breeding grounds: pelicans,
white egrets, royal terns, plovers, and coots—
their feathers and their young soak up the stain.

A swirl beneath the Gulf, like hurricane
Katrina, gathers strength in slow motion.
Eleven missing, and we have no name

for the muck on Grand Isle that eats through boots,
for come-and-go workers in hazmat suits.
Louisiana crude oil stains and stains and stains.
The search is ended. We pray their names.

Love Poem with Schooner and Ruins

You boys jailed yourselves for fun
smiling through rust-painted iron bars
the pamphlet says Geronimo was jailed
right here in Pensacola Bay at Fort Pickens
and now it is time to put heads in cannons
and in the cannon wasps and in my pocket
no Benadryl or Band-Aids just the camera
another picture without me in it unless
you were to count the shadow of my hat
a schooner will pass today on its way south
and then around the world while we wait we toss
black clods in the sand former pieces of road
Redneck Riviera on the rebound going on
four years since the hurricane undid our place
and this place where ants rope in and out
of cracks like blood through a troubled heart
do you remember the rental on Ariola
I aimed the spyglass the schooner a ghost
as pale as a frog's bones deeper in the Gulf
the rays soared beneath us tight as fighter planes
those Blue Angels that scare you with
flyovers and their roar out of nowhere
follow me boys walk behind rattlesnakes
I read are everywhere like landmines
forget the Hermit Crab Olympics for once
and get in the picture at the same time as the boat
earlier today I was an unkissed thing
attacked by terns while pedaling a rusty bike
but now each of you a hand in my hand I remember
your balancing act learning to walk
here's a poem do what you will ignore it
or let it be your thousandth paper airplane
annoying song stuck in your head love poem
with schooner and ruins and me blowing kisses
from everywhere and nowhere at once

Helicopter Hands

After the Katrina paintings of Rolland Golden

Among us one has named himself the hero boatman
of every canvas: *Somebody dreams of me when they painting.*
I hate to confess I'm more into their carrying on
than the Katrina paintings of Rolland Golden.
He paints to testify—flood stain eternal smeared
on shotgun houses, the color of a doomsday sunset,
but what about us, his subjects, a cast of thousands
with no speaking parts, and no names but the titles
he assigns, like *Helicopter Hands?* Not unlike Mardi Gras,
their shadowy reaches, their shouts and motions, all of it mute
to the man turning his back to walk inside and wait.
Next to me is someone's date in a rabbit fur coat
and too much glitter for a grandma. She drones on,
but I'm stuck on the fur coat that down here she wears
two times a year, tonight, tiny chill, being number one.
That's by my mama's house. We used to eat there after church.
Mystery coat, I let myself wonder if she bought it
with a FEMA check, though she could have packed it
in garbage bags before heading to her shelter of last resort,
the fur her one necessity besides Tijuana the cockatiel
and a box of Cheez-Its. I think she sees herself
as the woman he's got wading through the street
with a suitcase balanced on her hairdo. God bless.
He calls her *Headed for the Superdome*, and in the bag,
bulgy but invisible, all of her story, all of her wealth.

Katrina Scribendi

Oh, look—another gawker with some bullshit poems
about the hurricane. Just what we need,
our drama in real life reworked to be PC.
Yankeefied and chicken fried. Happy to oblige.
Let me guess—you came down for Mardi Gras
once and since Katrina you feel bad for us.
If not that, it had to be the Sugar Bowl,
plastic-cuffed by the can't-piss-in-public patrol.
You call your poems authentic in a heartfelt way,
but that rhyme on breathing in the stench of attic dead
is all pretend. Never happened outside your head.
Child's play poems. Imposters. Illegitimates.
I have an idea—let's put them to the test.
Awake, arise at once, all you FEMA trailer desperados,
and behold this book of grave robber poems.
It does the work for you, tells how you hacked
through shingles with a blunted axe.
Lady, I think we all agree—no better offering
to the red state south than your bedazzled poems.
What's that? I know. Ingrate—*c'est moi!* I should rejoice
that there exists a scribbling mob above the Mason-Dixon
moved to kick their voices my direction.
Rubberneckers, reckless and clever,
picking through my trash. You better never
let me catch you. The endless nerve,
a crown of sonnets promising, "This too shall pass."
I got one for you: Buzz off. Blow it out your ass.

Stupid Praise

One last Katrina poem, stupid praise for what I hated.
I quit. No more a guard dog of damaged goods
chained in the yard, drinking from tadpole puddles,
dragging my doom and gloom down happy streets.

I swear. No more damaged goods, watchdog groups,
or Katrina's white flags on the cemetery lawn.
No dragging doom and gloom down happy streets,
mistaking blue tarps in shreds for battered prayer flags.

Katrina's white flags on the cemetery lawn
in perfect lines marking the day and marking the dead—
consider them prayer flags, like blue tarps in shreds
announcing our surrender to the waterline.

No more jazz funerals or second line umbrellas, OK?
No more picking the scab, pressing in secret the bruise,
announcing our surrender to the waterline.
Katrina's footprint in the garage, let it fade.

Pick away at it—sweep up the muck and move on.
The world was just a dream of molded halls
and welcome mats, Katrina's footprint in the garage.
Ancient history to you, but always yesterday to me.

It was just a dream—the hallway, its ghost of mold,
crisscrossed downed power lines, and makeshift boats.
Yesterday feels like ancient history, the last page
in my notebook. I fill the lines and my hand shakes.

One last Katrina poem. Stupid praise for what I hated.

Invitation to the Gretna Royals

People, come see my new house. Make a day of it.
Ignore the voice in the car and make like your journey
is the scenic route to Beau Rivage Casino. Come at night
and let the moon lead the way. For your darling,
won't you cross Lake Pontchartrain? It's not jury duty.
Y'all can't stay mad, you clutch of poohbah wives
with gap teeth, and vanilla candle bathrooms,
and Buddha statue bookends. I'm still your daughter.
There's room enough in the big house for an altar
to all things Snoopy, for a locked-away shrine
of my father's wisdom, his back-of-the-toilet books.
Just come on. North of I-12 isn't Yankee north,
it's *Jahnke* north. Here there were Indian mounds
and ancient pines, now there be new construction.
The New Kountry—that's what they call it on the radio.
No real Bubbas other than attorneys who drive
fancy trucks. Fire tower. Goodwill. Kracklin' Skillet.
Answer my prayer for an escort into the pawn shop,
which is adjacent to the Wig and Hat shop where,
I bet, they sell Big Mama hose embroidered
with praying hands and *Thank You for the blood.*
Won't you come on? Here's one to make you laugh—
we have a septic tank that dribbles drinkable water
day and night to the ditch in front my house.
Tadpoles love it, but Yours Truly remains skeptical.
Other than that, for the most part, I fit in. Found a tick
on my neck and wore slippers to the gourmet grocery.
I promise to feed you white beans and shrimp
if you come. Just get in the car. So what if you don't know
the name of every beat cop and Winn Dixie cashier.
Take a break from the murders and windows with bars
and sit on my back porch instead. Quiet for miles.
Give a call when y'all get close. I'll shine my brights
on Lowe Davis Drive. I'll park there waiting for you
and then we'll caravan. It's not much farther.

Tabasco in Space

I hear a generator buzz, I taste those days,
citronella swirled with cardboard meals
and ice unlimited, and the welcome thrill
of Katrina's king cake dolls, half-ounce bottles
of Tabasco packed with MREs marked
"Chicken Fajitas." People thought our food
was special made, a little heat singing
to the tongue of home, but I knew better.
Long have the McIlhennys been men in arms,
and Tabasco has always traveled with them,
from saddlebags, to officers' tables,
to the final frontier—Tabasco in space,
floating from the dripper to the spaceman's lip.

What could be more American than
a Yankee banker ruined by the Civil War
come south to make it big with pepper sauce?

My worst job, worse than Taco Bell cashier,
was at Hill Memorial, a special collections library,
where it fell to me to tackle patrons fool enough
to sneak a pencil in the reading room.
Afternoons I worked behind the scenes
sorting donations, mostly major donor
McIlhenny stuff, his great-grands dumping crates
of a rich life's ticket stubs and corsages.

The librarians couldn't flat out refuse,
which meant shelf space dog-eared in the stacks
for resin hummingbird statuettes alongside
Audubon's *Wild Turkey,* collectible most high,
and print number one in *Birds of America.*
Protocol demanded white gloves, as on butlers of yore,
be worn when turning the folio pages

with tissue paper in between meant to keep
the reds from fading, red berries and beaks
living mostly in the archived dark.

They didn't end well, my library months.
I got so tired of filing letters to the world,
letters meant for home, the family bible's
apocrypha intercepted, transcribed, and shellacked.
Moss Madonna decoupage, and photographs
of slaves around the sugar pot, the children
battling stillness so hard that in the aftermath,
to history, they're just a blur.

I wonder
when they noticed my long, long lunch,
my blazer left behind on its peg, work
unfinished on the desk like an exhibit
at the Gallier House, all but the threshold
of the room roped off. If only I'd have thought
to tease them with a prank, something harmless,
like sharpening the golf pencils at both ends,
little footprints, Tabasco bottles placed
at random in the stacks—near Kingfish's
windbag letters, between gilt books in cages.
A fake collection, "The Hot Stuff Chronicles"—
among its contents a list of nonfood uses:
sentry-watch eye drops, cure-all for a sassy tongue.

Tabasco released a C-ration cookbook
as a joke. Somebody sent me one
in a letter not long ago—did they jest,
or fear I'd turned survivalist after a peek
at my post-Katrina stash? So many ways
to spend a mouthful of vinegar and smoke.
Maybe I am crazy—awaiting the end of days,
except for me and mine, who'll be hydrated and fed,
dressed in desert fatigues, and off the grid.

Notes

Gretna appears in several of the poems. It is where I grew up, a city on the west bank of the Mississippi River and forever in the shadow of New Orleans.

In "Daughter of the Confederacy" the words "Farbys" and "thread counters" refer to overzealous Civil War reenactors.

"Our Lady of Prompt Succor" is another name for Mary, the blessed virgin and patroness of the city of New Orleans. Many pray to her during hurricane season in general, particularly when there is a storm in the Gulf.

"The Day the Music Stopped" refers to a silent march that took place on the second anniversary of Katrina in protest of the slow pace of recovery in New Orleans.

The McIlhennys referred to in the poem "Tabasco in Space" are the family who invented the famed pepper sauce Tabasco. Tabasco was originated by Edmund McIlhenny, as he was looking to add some flavor to the bland food of the reconstruction south.

The Kingfish is a nickname for Huey P. Long, former governor of Louisiana.